# A Life of St. W

### St Werburgh of Chester

## Matthew E. Pointon

Lord, Your servant Werburgh turned her back on wealth, privilege and power and entered into a closer union with You.
Help me to reject all the false gods of self-interest, affluence and personal power to serve you and my fellow human beings.
Lord, Werburgh grew in holiness and became a shining light for Your presence and grace.
Help me through prayer to grow in Your knowledge and love, that I too may shine in the world to Your glory.
Lord, Werburgh was lose to You in Your creation. Help to respect and reverence all that You have made and to work in harmony with Your creative will.
Lord, Werburgh became a beacon of hope, of healing, and of renewal to your people who still come to honour her example at her shrine.
May I find this day wholeness of mind, body and spirit and a new resolution to serve You by bringing Your love to others.
This I ask in the name of our Lord, Jesus Christ.
AMEN

*Prayer for St. Werburgh*

# Prologue

The wind whistled through the trees and the rain plastered the girl's hair against her cheeks. Was it the rain though, or was it instead her tears which fell continuously from her eyes, eyes that stared unblinking at the scene before them.

There was a figure lain on the floor bloodied and broken. Beside that figure knelt a lady sobbing silently, cradling the head of the dead boy, her tears falling into his lifeless eyes. It reminded the girl of another scene, far, far away, a long time ago, a scene that she had pondered over many times as she'd sat beside that lady who was now lamenting just as Mary had once done. That lady, her mother, the most wonderful lady ever to have lived since that equally tragic mourning Mother at Golgotha.

At Golgotha Mary had cradled her dead son but others had been present then, stood back, each engrossed in their own thoughts. So it had been then and so it was now, and try as she might, the girl could neither step nearer to the slain innocent yet nor could she leave. She could not leave for he was her brother, her youngest brother whom she'd loved dearly, whom she'd played with as a child, laughed with, argued with, fought with, shared her very life with. She could not leave she loved him so and could not bear to think of him as gone, never to return. It had been hard when they'd found her other brother, Wulfad, but at least then had been some hope that Rufin would survive, that he would make it, that he would escape. But now even that hope was extinguished and all that remained was a dark night which seemed as if it would stretch for all eternity.

And that night was so very dark because she could do nothing to lighten it, she could not draw nearer to comfort her distraught mother, she could not the evils that had been committed. Evils that had been committed because of her. If it hadn't been for her they'd both still be alive, they'd still all be one big happy family. It was her fault, all her fault, her fault for being so pretty yet so headstrong, so selfish in her wants. If she hadn't been here then they wouldn't be dead and...

She raised her fists and started hitting her head, grabbing at her long golden tresses and tearing them out. If she was no longer beautiful, if she was bruised and broken like that innocent boy lying there then no one else would have to die, everything would be alright, everything...

A pair of hands grasped hers and pulled her to the embrace of a warm woollen cloak. Defeated, dejected, she buried herself into the cloth, sobbing uncontrollably. So what if it was him, that odious snake who had caused all this? She no longer cared, nothing mattered anymore. She sobbed and she sobbed until she could sob no more and he held her tight the whole while. Then, when she finally stopped, he wiped her face and said softly, "Fear not for all shall be well again."

She looked up. That was not *his* voice; that was not *his* face. It was the voice and the face of another, another whom she knew well. A man as different in character and calling to *him* as there could be.

"It is not your fault," he said softly.

"But they died because he told my father and he only did that because he was angry because..."

"Hush, hush. True or not, it is still not your fault."

"But..."

"No 'buts', you did what was right, they did what was right. Only your father and him..."

"Evil men! I hate them! I hate them both with all my heart, yet one is my father who gave me life and the other his most trusted friend!"

"Shh! Their deeds were evil, not them. Hate the sin, not the sinner. As you yourself are angry now, they too were angry and anger compels us to do the most terrible things."

"But I too am angry with them, with myself, with this cruel unfair world!"

"Then fight that anger and ask God to help you in that fight. Anger has no place here: this terrible scene before our eyes should remind us what happens when we submit to anger."

She looked at her mother and the corpse of her brother. Yes, answer was not the answer, it is never the answer. Her mother had stopped weeping now and was piling stones over the body.

"Go help her," said Chad. "She needs you at this time and the Lord will need you after that. Take this stone Werburgh and begin building a shrine in memory of your martyred brothers."

---

Christ had been a part of Werburgh's life since before she could remember. Indeed, her earliest memory was of her sitting on her mother's lap in the tower room as Ermenilda told her stories from the Bible. Indeed, by the time she was eight years old she knew all about Abraham, Moses and the Ten Commandments, Joseph and his coat, Jeremiah, Jacob and his ladder, the journeyings of St. Paul, the Exile in Babylon, Elijah on the mountainside, the bravery of Esther, the humility of Mary and the love of Jesus Christ.

All this was possible, she later realised, because she was a girl. Although he loved her in his own way, at a very early age Werburgh had realised that she was not as important to King Wulfhere as her two younger brothers. That was because, as a girl, she was not an heir, she would leave the family one day, she would never inherit the kingdom. And as a girl, and thus unimportant, the king paid little attention to what his wife taught their daughter. With Wulfad and Rufin however, things were very different and ever since he had assumed the throne, Wulfhere had forbidden his queen to talk to their sons about Jesus and the saints for they would one day inherit Mercia and Mercia was Pagan.

Queen Ermenilda's great disappointment in life was her husband. Whilst the rest of the world admired him for his courage, his prowess in battle and his rugged masculinity – "A true Saxon!" they would declare – she merely despaired for his soul. She despaired over the fact that he had accepted baptism when the Northumbrians were in control – and indeed her father had only married his favourite daughter to this rough and ready Mercian prince because he had seen it as a way of ensuring that Mercia remained Christian – but had then rejected that baptism and reverted to the old Pagan ways. She despaired even more though over the fact that neither the baptism, when the Christian Northumbrians held power, nor the sudden reversal back to the old faith, when he needed allies against the Northumbrians, had been real conversions of any kind; both had been motivated by power alone and God had never played a role in King Wulfhere's life beyond the ceremonial. And that, in meek and mild Ermenilda's eyes, made him only half a man.

So whilst Werburgh had grown up in the love of Christ, her brothers and playmates had not. And as they had evolved from boys into adolescents, they had taunted and teased her over her devotion to her weak and feminine god who meekly went to a criminal's death and who contrasted poorly with the mighty Woden and Thor.

But then one fateful day all that changed, They'd rode off to hunt on their horses in the morning and when they returned late in the evening they'd come to her and begged her forgiveness for the nasty and cruel things that they'd said. And as they did their faces glowed with an almost serene light and Werburgh realised that her two brothers were men transformed.

# *Part I*

If Christ had been a figure always present in her life, Werbode was one that had only really entered it of late but had wrought much havoc and misery during the short time that he had been there.

Like Christ, Werbode had in fact always been present but during her years as a girl he had never even noticed her existence which, since she was a female, was entirely understandable since she was of no consequence unlike Werbode himself who was of great consequence indeed being father's finest general and most trusted right-hand man. However, just over a year ago, soon after her bleeding had started and her breasts begun to grow, he had suddenly started to notice her more and more and would always make a beeline to pay her a compliment or kiss her on the cheek. This had been slightly tiresome but no great issue until that fateful day when her father had summoned her to his chamber where she'd found him waiting with Werbode.

Wulfhere had smiled and asked her how she was and after she'd replied that she was well he'd enquired, "Tell me dearest daughter, how are you disposed towards this man here, my most trusted servant, Werbode?"

She'd looked at that man of similar years to her father and still unsuspecting had replied, "He is your friend, father, and so I like and respect him also."

"And more than that?"

"I don't comprehend your meaning, father?"

"I shall put it plainly daughter: Werbode here has today asked my permission for your hand and I have granted it gladly for you could have no finer husband in all Mercia than he. So darling Werburgh, how stand you for marriage?"

Marriage! A husband! Werbode! No! No! No! She felt as if the earth had opened up and she was falling down a bottomless chasm. Marry... she could not, for she had already pledged herself to another, to a man far greater than Werbode!

Tears ran down her face. "No sir, I cannot!" she declared running from the room.

"Don't worry friend, she is young, she shall come round," King Wulfhere reassured his friend.

---

"Mother, I need to talk."

"Come daughter, what is it?"

"Today father summoned me. He asked me how I stand to marry."

"I know. And how do you stand?"

"I stand well but..."

"But...?"

"But not to Werbode, another, not to Werbode!"

"Why not child? They say that he is one of the greatest warriors in all Mercia, a fine upstanding man and handsome too."

"Perhaps so mother, but I cannot love him."

"Werburgh, if you have love in a marriage at the very start then that is indeed a great blessing from the Lord, but do not fear if you don't for it shall come as it did with your father and me, with time."

"But mother, I love another!"

"Another?!"

"Yes mother, another."

"And is this other as good, as brave and as manly as Werbode?"

"He is all that and more."

"And does your father approve of him?"

"No mother, he definitely does not."

"Then neither do I, for your father is my lord and master and we are of one mind!"

"No mother, you are not. My father is not your lord and master and your minds, thankfully, are not one!"

"Werburgh, how can you say such things?!"

"I say them because I know that you approve of my match dearest mother, you approve with all of your heart. For it was you who introduced me to this man whilst I was still in my cradle, you who let Him enter my chamber every night, you who bade me talk to Him, walk with Him and to trust and believe in Him completely."

"Werburgh, do I understand you correctly? You wish to marry Him, that one man greater than all others?!"

"He is calling me mother!"

"Your father will never agree!"

"Nonetheless, He still calls me. What am I to do? Where is my hope?"

"In Him my daughter, in Him."

---

That grave looks different now to how it did then. True, the stones are piled just as they were then, but there is moss and grass between them now and they are dry today. All is dry now for the sun shines brightly in the sky, its rays shimmering through the leaves of the trees and illuminating the two figures knelt beside those stones.

"Even now I still ask 'Why'?"

"The Lord moves in mysterious ways, Werburgh."

"But why did they have to die?"

"Why did they have to die? Because for change to come about sometimes a sacrifice is needed. What was the first consequence of Adam and Eve being cast out of the Garden? They needed clothing and feeding. Which animal died to provide those clothes and food? An innocent just like your brother Rufin, your other saintly brother Wulfad and like Him."

Silence reigns between them, two souls immersed in the Divine.

"That night I thought that all was lost and that I was the cause of it all. You know it was Werbode who told my father that they had become Christians and he only did that because I had rejected his advances in favour of a betrothal to Christ. He must have hated Christ so much for causing him such anguish."

"Anger and jealousy can destroy even the best of men, as too can the temptation of power."

"And my own father, how could I ever love him again after he had slain his own children with his own hand?"

"As I said, anger, power and temptation can destroy even the best of men. Think of David when he viewed Bathsheba. But like David your father has repented and like David, God has heard his prayers. And like Christ Himself, your brothers Rufin and Wulfad did not die in vain for through their blood the entire Kingdom of Mercia has turned back to Christ; through their blood your father has been reborn a better and purer man and it is through their blood that you can now marry whom you desire and your mother can find peace and fulfilment."

"I have never seen her happier than when my brother Bertram was born only nine months after the stag led my father to you and he embraced Christ once again."

"Bertram is a blessing from God, Werburgh, and I have no doubt that in time he shall prove that to the world."

As she stared at those stones and listened to the words of Holy Chad, Werburgh cast her mind back to her father's anguish after his anger had subsided and the wine wore off, to how he beat himself and tore his hair by the banks of the Trent, to how he rode off into the forest and the stag led him to the hermit whom he then knelt before and begged both his and his God's forgiveness for the terrible crimes that he had committed and of how Chad had laid his hand on the king's head and told him softly that all his sins had been forgiven. And she remembered too her mother's face when she had learnt of that joyous conversion.

"They died for me," Werburgh said slowly to Chad, "and so it is my duty now to ensure that I was worthy of such a sacrifice."

# Part II

The weather that day was as wretched as it had been on that terrible day when she'd stood by the corpse of her brother, but her mood was now much harder to discern. On the surface she was miserable, scared, lonely, a pitiful figure swathed in cloth peering out from between the folds at the desolate landscape before her, barren hills lashed by the anger of a dark grey sky, bolts of lightning from the heavens illuminating the path before her as if warning of the hell that lay ahead.

Inside though, deep within her breast, nestled another feeling, well hidden and protected but there nonetheless. It was a feeling of joy and hope, the feeling of the impending realisation of a lifelong dream.

In her entire life Werburgh had never travelled further than a few hours ride from the great fortress of Wulfherecester[1] which had been her hope since birth. Now though, she was on her third day on the road and many more lay ahead, more days of cold that chills the bones, rain that soaks through to the skin, soreness and aching bones from days on horseback and terror, terror borne of the fact that the next spinney, wood or forest might contain a gang of bandits who could easily overpower her two-man escort and then carry her off to her death... or an even worse fate.

Yet all of this was necessary, this long, long journey across a world that she had never before realised was so big. After two days she'd thought that they must have passed Ely already and be halfway to Rome yet when the guard showed her how little distance they had covered she was shocked. Yes indeed, this world is vast; God is even greater than she'd thought.

She fortified herself with that story from her childhood, the story of a young woman, not dissimilar in age to herself who was forced to travel on a donkey all the way to Bethlehem and, when she thought of it, she was glad for in comparison her lot was an easy one. Unlike Mary she had chosen to undertake this journey; unlike Mary she had the luxury of a horse; unlike Mary she didn't have the pain and incapacity of a swollen belly to cope with and unlike

---

[1] Burybank

Mary, she knew that at the end of it all she had a welcome, a room and a warm bed waiting for her. Unlike Mary she was blessed indeed!

That bed was in the great Abbey of Ely overseen by her great aunt Æthelthryth, one of the holiest women in the land, and it represented the marriage that she so yearned for; marriage to a divine, not earthly spouse, the taking of the veil and becoming a Bride of Christ. It was the realisation of her dream, a dream made possible after her father's conversion, after the martyrdom of her two saintly siblings. "Wulfad and Rufin, my dear brothers in Heaven, plead on my behalf that I may survive this perilous journey so that I may serve Christ fully to the end of my days and in doing so make worthy your sacrifices." As she prayed the cold rain continued to lash down on her cheeks yet somehow, inside, she felt warm and dry.

# Part III
## *Twenty-four years later*

Her eyes stared at the cross. The simple wooden cross upon which hung the Saviour of the world. She stared at it intently, drinking in all its joy, hope, mystery and power. Tears dripped from her eyes but as with the last time we met her, those tears betray not one, but a multitude of emotions. Emotions known only to He who had hung on that cross.

Werburgh is different now, ten years older and her dazzling beauty has faded somewhat to be replaced by an air of wisdom and piety achievable only through age and prayer. Would she have looked the same had she accepted Werbode's proposal all those years ago? What would her life have been like? Joy through motherhood and devotion to her temporal but not divine lord and master? Or instead misery, the misery that comes of not following one's destiny? Perhaps other miseries too? Mourning over dead children as her mother had had to endure? Or perhaps death visiting her personally during the unbearable agony of childbirth?

Yet all the while she knew that this was not about her, it was all about something far greater. She'd been a royal princess then and her refusal of Werbode had led to the martyrdom of two saints, her own beloved brothers. Yet that martyrdom had itself led to a king, and thus his kingdom's, conversion, the winning of a holy people for Christ. Werburgh imagined a Mercia still Pagan. It was an empty, soulless vision. Yes indeed, this had always been about much more than just her.

Her meditations then switched to that long and dangerous journey, the frightened girl on horseback venturing forth to a fate unknown in a far-off land. She recalled that unceasing rain, the stinging, biting wind and then, up ahead, the flickering lights of Ely. She remembered the large wooden doors opening and her great aunt embracing her. "You are home now," was all that she had said and it was true for Ely was her home now far more than Wulfherecester had ever been. She had not left it since that day, she had spent her hours in prayer, meditation, labouring in the vegetable gardens and laundry, on her knees as now in her rude cell furnished only with a straw bed and a cross. The cross that she now stared at with such devotion; the cross that had witnessed her transform slowly but surely from a timid teenage novice to a strong woman, the Abbess of Ely no less.

Yet today was the last time that she would see that cross or indeed the entire abbey that had become her home. A message had arrived from Mercia that morning. Messages rarely arrived from her former home; during the entire twenty years spent as a Bride of Christ she could count the messages that she'd received on one hand. The first had informed her that her younger brother Bertram had renounced the world and become a hermit; the second that her father had died and Bertram had repelled the Northumbrian foes of Mercia with the help of Christ whilst the third, which arrived soon after the second, told her that her mother was on her way to join her as a nun at Ely. Her mother arrived and, when her grandmother Seaxburgh, the Second Abbess of Ely passed away to the Lord, Ermenilda took over as the Third Abbess. This fourth message though was unlike all the others; it was a summons from her uncle Æthelred, the new king of Mercia, commanding her to return to her place of birth immediately.

But how? How could she leave this place which she loved so much, where she was fully immersed in the work of God. "Please Father, take this cup away from me!" she cried inwardly. Yet even as she pleaded, she knew. The Lord showed her a garden, a garden newly planted with flowers. Yet the plants were young and weak and both weeds and wild animals lurked menacingly whilst the sun shone brightly overhead making them call out for water. "This is your garden," said the Lord. "Your brothers planted the seeds, now you must tend to the flowers." Werburgh understood then that Mercia, not Ely, was her garden and she thanked the Lord for His wisdom and mercy. Then she rose from her knees and prepared to depart.

---

Stepping back inside the precincts of Wulfherecester was an unnerving, almost surreal experience for Werburgh. On the one hand it was all so familiar, this was her childhood home, she knew every square inch of it. It was where she had played and slept, where she'd grown from a tiny crying mite in her mother's arms into a defiant young woman intent on marrying her Saviour. Every building, every tree, every sight, sound and smell she recognised and all brought back potent memories.

Yet at the same time it was also all so very different. That mother who had raised her was gone and so too was her father, interred within a mound that dominated the crest of an adjacent hill. There were new faces abroad and a new king on the throne, but most changed of all was herself; she saw things with different eyes now and looked upon the young girl who'd once played hide and seek with her brothers within those walls as a separate person entirely, as if she were watching an entertainment put on by some travelling players.

One familiar figure though, was the man who now sat on the throne of Mercia, her uncle, Æthelred, the one who had summoned her. When he saw her enter he jumped up from his seat and rushed to greet her. They embraced in silence as all the memories of her Mercian childhood flocked back to her and then he ordered all his nobles and retainers to leave. And when they were alone he spoke:

"Werburgh, I have summoned you here to undertake a great commission and I trust that you will accept it."

"Uncle, I can only accept what is God's Will. I was happy at Ely and..."

"Shh! Hear me out! Almost twenty five years ago this great kingdom reverted to the Christian faith through the ministrations of Holy Chad, through the pure heart of your own blessed mother, through the martyrdom of your saintly brothers Wulfad and Rufin and through the conversion of your father. Mercia is again Christian and for that we should give thanks, but the battle is, I am sorry to say, but half won. People pay homage to the faith with their lips but I fear that in their hearts they are still as pagan as they ever were. Yes, they come to your younger brother Bertram for healing, but I fear that they are more in love with his miracles than the God which allows him to perform them. The fact is, aside from Chad's priory at Licidfelth[2] and the priory that was set up at the place of your brother Wulfad's martyrdom, there is no one in this land to propagate the Gospel and spread the faith of Christ so that it may truly enter the hearts of the Mercians, and, as king of this land, that disturbs me no end and causes me to toss and turn

---

[2] Lichfield

and lose sleep at night. So it was that I asked for God's guidance and so it was that He gave me your name Werburgh. 'The child that entered the abbey at Ely is now a woman and ready to do My work.' And so it was that I summoned you here."

"Uncle, I do not understand."

"Werburgh, do you not see? Mercia has a father but she needs a mother as well, to nourish her children with her spiritual milk. She needs a spiritual queen who can bring Christ into her people's hearts. You were once a princess of this land, now you can become so much more. I shall grant you land where you ask for it and money to found priories, centres of the Christian faith that can reach out and bless every household in the kingdom. I have summoned you here Werburgh, to become the Mother of Mercia."

"No! No! Uncle, you have got it wrong! I am not the one that God named. There are many saintly sisters at Ely who were once girls, but I am not one of them. I am just a poor, flawed nun trying to serve Christ in the simplest fashion that she can. Remember uncle, I ran away from power to the abbey; I do not seek such honours, they are for others far better qualified than I am!"

"Werburgh, dearest Werburgh, there is no one on this earth better qualified for this task than you. It is your very humility and disinterest in temporal power that makes you the ideal candidate for the Lord would never have chosen one who sought such honours for it is well know that those who seek power become corrupted by it. The people have always loved their beautiful princess, daughter of their most beautiful and saintly queen, yet they love her all the more now for tales of her piety and humble nature are commonplace here. Your children see you Werburgh, your Lord has chosen you: shall you answer their call?"

Still did she long to refuse but as the king spoke that image of a garden threatened by weeds and wild beasts returned. Yes, she was needed here, the Lord *had* chosen her. "I accept, sire," she said quietly with a bowed head.

---

Werburgh started in her mission by marrying her childhood with her adult life. She chose a spot almost within sight of Wulfherecester called Trenthamm,[3] on the peaceful banks of the infant Trent, that graceful river that had witnessed her childhood games as well as the tragic ends of the lives of the two elder brothers that had shared them. Then she sent word to Ely requesting, in the name of the great King Æthelred, some of those sisters whom she knew to be well-suited to such pioneering work. When they arrived several weeks later, she embraced Sisters Wulfryn, Æmma and Cwenburgh warmly, those pious witnesses to her adult life in the abbey and fellow brides of Christ. Then they began the difficult work of establishing the priory. Whilst the labourers were still erecting its humble wooden church and outbuildings, Werburgh decided upon Sister Wulfryn to be her prioress and then assisted her in selecting young novices from the local community.

Choosing Sister Wulfryn had been no easy task. She had always been much closer to Sister Æmma who was her age and as pious and dedicated as any nun in Christendom. Sister Wulfryn on the other hand, had always been a little too stern for her tastes but Werburgh recognised that whilst Sister Æmma possessed many Christ-like qualities, she could not command the respect or attention of the other sisters, for she allowed everything and reprimanded no one so that even the pious took advantage of her good nature.

Sister Cwenburgh however, did command both respect and attention and had very firm boundaries in what she deemed to be acceptable. But in Werburgh's mind, with her those boundaries were, if anything, far too firm and rigid and they left little room for the forgiveness that Christ preached so beautifully. Werburgh realised, for the first time in her life, the responsibilities that come with power. As a girl, as a novice and as a nun, she had had always followed; followed her father, followed her mother, followed the Rule, followed the instructions of the Abbess, followed Christ. Now though, she had to lead, to pick and then send disciples out into the world just as Christ had sent His Apostles out to every city and place whither he himself was about to come. She dearly wanted to grant her good friend Æmma the position of honour at Trenthamm[3], but her prayers, head and heart told her that to do so would only court disaster. A leader must be appointed on the basis of suitability, not friendship.

---

[3] Trentham

Whilst the walls were still rising at Trenthamm and the fields around the priory still being sowed, Werburgh was off again, for her mission was not to establish one house but many. Still, it pained her heart to leave, for she longed to see the project that she had so enthusiastically started come to its completion, but she knew now that her fate was that of St. Paul of Tarsus, not St. Anthony of Egypt. Æthelred had promised her many more sites but not all were suitable; some were too marshy, others in areas already quite Christianised, others still too rocky or indefensible if attacked. So she found herself travelling far and wide, all over the kingdom, tiring days on horseback, another sea change for the lady who had spent the best part of the last three decades cloistered inside a single compound. But whilst she at first missed her beloved abbey at Ely and longed for those long hours of silent contemplation, day by day she slowly began to revel in her new life, in the joys of looking outwardly, not inwards, indulging in the glories of the wonderful world that God has created.

The change in her attitude really shifted after she'd journeyed up into the northern hills to visit the site of the hermitage of her younger brother Bertram, near to which Æthelred had offered some land on which to found a priory.

Bertram and her youngest brother Cœnrad, were the siblings that Werburgh had never really known, born to her mother after the deaths of Wulfad and Rufin. Bertram should have become king after Wulfhere's death, but instead, at a young age he had travelled to the Kingdom of Mide where he had met, fell in love and eloped with a princess of that place. God however, had punished them for their sins for upon returning to Mercia, whilst he had been away seeking a midwife for his pregnant love, a wolf had ravaged both the girl and her newly-born child. Distraught with grief and his own guilt, her brother had, like her, dedicated his life to God and gone on to be a hermit, miracle man and healer. As they sat together by the gentle waters of the Manifold and Bertram had told her all about the Christ he saw in the mountains, trees and stones, and in the faces and hearts of the humble peasants who came to him for blessings, Werburgh realised that whilst there was much to be said of withdrawing from the world, the Lord also calls us to be part of it. After all, Christ, the example to us all, not only fasted in the desert for forty days and nights; upon his return he then preached the Sermon on the Mount.

But Bertram's path and hers, whilst both ordained by the same God, were not the same and Æthelred was surprised by her reply when he asked her upon her return from that place when she wished to found a priory by the Manifold.

"No sire, there shall be no priory in that place for there is no need of one. At the spot where the Dove and the Manifold meet, the Lord has built His own temple of rock, earth and water and my holy brother Bertram is its priest. The Lord already moves in that place, I do not need to put Him there. Instead, I have followed the river downstream and selected a different spot, at a place called Heánbyrig,[4] above the banks of the Dove on the crest of a hill. It has views stretching all the way up to those northern hills, but it is master of a fertile plain. That is the place where the Lord wishes me to build His priory.

---

Word came to Werburgh that there was a sister at Ely who dearly wished to become the Prioress of the new establishment at Heánbyrig. Her name was Friðugyth and Werburgh knew her slightly as she had been a novice whilst Werburgh was there. Furthermore, she was also of royal birth so Werburgh decided to send for her. Upon arrival at Trenthamm – where Werburgh had her base – she held an audience with her. An hour later, when the audience had finished, her heart was greatly confused. Sister Friðugyth had many admirable qualities – enthusiasm, zeal, Christ in her heart and a kindly nature – but Werburgh worried that she was still too young and inexperienced to fulfil such a role. "But she so greatly wishes to serve you!" she told the Lord in her prayers that evening. But what is it that she wants so much? Power? Fame? The chance to do My work? Justification of her own high opinion of herself? Werburgh realised that this was a test and so the following morning she called Sister Friðugyth in.

"Sister, you impressed me greatly yesterday and I have prayed much over the matter. I have sent for Sister Lufe from Ely. She is a pious and experienced nun and ideal for the post of Prioress at Heánbyrig. However, she is aged and will need your help. Would you therefore consent to being her deputy?"

---

[4] Hanbury

Sister Friðugyth's face fell, but she said nothing, only looked heavenwards, seeking guidance from Him. Then she spoke: "I shall not pretend not to be disappointed but I trust your wisdom and His wisdom above all else and I believe that I can do just as much good as a deputy to Sister Lufe who is, as you say, an able and saintly nun, as I could as a prioress myself." With those words Werburgh knew that Sister Friðugyth had passed the test and sure enough, a year later when Sister Lufe retired to Ely, Sister Friðugyth became prioress at Heánbyrig, a role in which she excelled for many years.

# Part IV

Heánbyrig now safe and established, Werburgh then set out again, traversing the kingdom from north to south, east to west, setting up new priories or visiting and invigorating old ones. As the weeks passed tales of this princess who had forsaken all worldly wealth for the treasures of Heaven grew and grew and the people flocked to see her, asking her to bless their babies or to cure the afflicted. Whilst she longed for nothing more than to be left alone to pray and get on with her mission, she realised, just as her brother Bertram had taught her, that these outpourings were manifestations of the Holy Spirit and symbolic of the slow but sure conversion of Mercia to Christ, and so she welcomed them and with each smile, laying on of hands or kind word from her lips, her fame grew and the people loved her all the more.

She next established a priory at Triccingham far to the east and then Weedon in the south and it was whilst she was working in that place that a most incredible event took place. She was knelt at her prayers one day when Wilnoðe, a young and excitable novice, burst in on her. "Holy mother! Come quick!" she cried. "There's a great commotion!"

The 'commotion' was being caused by a large flock of wild geese which were ravaging the fields that the sisters had planted with vegetables. Werburgh strode up to them with the true authority of a leader and tried to shoo them off but they would not budge. Then she tried to round them up but they wouldn't obey. She tried again but again nothing happened, they were staying put for these were wild geese after all. "Oh Lord, give me strength!" she prayed inwardly and to her astonishment the birds obeyed immediately and, with little trouble at all, she and the other sisters and servants herded them all into an empty barn.

That night she lay awake in her cell thinking. What did it mean? She had been unable to control the geese on her own yet merely asking God and they'd obeyed her completely! It was a miracle, a quiet, secret miracle that only she and the Lord were aware of, but it was a miracle nonetheless, a demonstration of His omnipotence. Yet how come she had been granted the ability to perform miracles? Holy men and saints like Chad and Bertram performed miracles, not people like her, a mere woman, a mere simple and sinful woman. And why? Why had God granted her this power? All things have a purpose, that she knew, but what was His purpose in this?

She awoke just before five for Lauds and then went down to the barn containing the geese. Emboldened by her God-given powers from the previous night, she flung the door wide open and declared firmly, "You must leave now!"

But the geese did not leave. They did not even stir.

"Go! Shoo! In the Lord's name, fly away!" she commanded, rushing into the barn clapping her hands.

But they did not go, nor shoo, nor fly away. Instead they stood their ground and hissed and cackled.

Werburgh stopped. What was the meaning of this? Why had the Lord deserted her just as unexpectedly as he had come to her aid but a day before? Then she remembered, she recalled Elijah on the mountainside and that still, small voice.

She stopped and listened to those hisses and cackles and as she listened those cries of dumb beasts formed themselves into words, human speech. It was another miracle and another that only she was aware of. "We can't leave!" they cried. "We won't leave! One of our brothers is missing!"

"One of your brothers is missing? How?"

The servants and the nuns listening to her talking to these wildfowl in amazement: had the holy mother gone mad?!

"that man there by the door, he took him last night and he has not returned him!"

"I shall see what I can do."

Werburgh turned to the bemused onlookers and pointed to the servant stood by the doorpost. "You boy! Did you take one of these geese last night?"

"Well Holy Mother, the thing is I..."

"A simple answer will suffice: yes or no?"

He cast his eyes to the floor. "Yes Holy Mother."

"Then bring it back here!"

"But..."

"Bring it here!"

The boy ran off and returned some minutes later with the goose, or to be more precise, the half-eaten carcass of the bird. When they saw it the flock of wildfowl let out an almighty lament of cackles and hisses. Werburgh however, merely raised her arms and shouted, "Silence!" The method in the Lord's thinking was clear to her now.

An unnatural hush fell upon the scene. Geese watching from one side, humans from the other and in the centre, Werburgh with the remains of the dead bird. Slowly and silently she knelt down beside it, placed her hands over it and muttered, "Thy Will be done!" and then bending down further, she kissed it on the head.

A head that then moved, only slightly it is true, but a movement nonetheless. And when she raised herself she revealed to the onlooking crowd a whole and healthy bird. The resurrected goose stretched out its wings, looked around in astonishment and then went to join its brethren.

An almighty chorus of cackles filled the air, cackles to everyone but Werburgh. To her though, they were cries of heartfelt thanks. "Thank you! Thank you! Thank you Holy Mother! How can we ever repay you?"

"Leave this place and plague our fields no more!"

And in an almighty flurry of wings, the flock flew off into the air and left and never since have wild geese troubled the fields of Weedon Priory.

Then Werburgh turned to the servant boy. "Are you a Christian?" she asked.

"Y-y-yes Holy Mother."

"Then do you not know the commandment 'Thou shalt not steal'?"

"Yes Holy Mother, I do know it and I'm sorry, I..."

"Do you truly repent?"

"In the name of Christ Jesus I do, I truly do!"

"Then go and sin no more."

## Part V

It never ceased to amaze Werburgh that the episode with the geese caused her far more fame – and did Christ's cause far more good – than all of her other endeavours put together. Founding priories where souls were prayed for, the sick tended, the poor fed and the Gospel spread paled into nothing in the eyes of the simple folk of Mercia beside being able to talk with dumb beasts and resurrect one insignificant goose from the dead. She understood now why Christ had granted her brother the ability to transform bread into stones and why He Himself had transformed water into wine, multiplied loaves and fishes and walked on water. Miracles translate the Gospel into a language that all can understand and whilst they may seem rather meaningless acts in their own right – one less goose in the world, a thousands who listened to Christ have to wait a little longer for their meal – they contain far greater and deeper truths than that, truths which can be far more powerfully understood than if they had been preached in the churches. Christ's miracle of the loaves and fishes showed that God does not let His people go hungry; her resurrection of that humble goose demonstrated that each one of His creatures is precious to its Creator, no matter how humble it may be.

Now, wherever she went, Werburgh was feted and welcomed like the princess that she had fled from becoming. But her popularity boosted the cause of Christ; young women streamed to the gates of the new priories that she established eager to become Brides of Christ whilst rich families donated wood, gold and labour for their construction. And so the Church now flourished across Mercia and as Werburgh felt old age begin to approach, she realised that she had fulfilled the holy duty that King Æthelred – and the King of Heaven Himself – had entrusted her with: the Gospel had now truly entered the hearts of the Mercians.

But then, just as she realised that what she had come to do had been done and she could therefore now relax a little, God in His infinite wisdom decided to test her again. A test in the shape of a letter that was delivered to her as she prayed in her beloved priory at Heánbyrig. The message that it contained was short but overwhelming:

*My dear Sister in Christ,*

*I regret to inform you that the Abbess of Ely, your dear lady mother, has passed on to the Heavenly Realm. I therefore summon you to return to your abbey as you are required to take over her role.*

*Yours in Christ*

*Hildaburgh †*

Of course Werburgh had been kept up to speed with events at Ely. After her great aunt Æthelthryth had passed away, her grandmother Seaxburgh had taken over and then after she herself had died, then holy Ermenilda, her beloved mother had become Abbess. IT was only natural therefore that she should be the next to fill that exalted seat, but to abandon her work in Mercia... now that was a blow.

A blow almost as harsh as losing her darling mother who had nurtured her from birth, loved her as only a mother can and been to Werburgh as Our Lady had been to Christ. Unseen by all save the Lord, she wept many tears that night as she prayed.

---

The long journey down to Ely was far more taxing for the older Werburgh than it had been for the younger all those years before and by the time she arrived at the gates she was ill with the fever. The worried sisters feared that their new abbess might pass on to the Lord even before she had been invested so they took her to the best cell and tended her with great love and care, and after resting for several weeks she recovered and was able to commence her duties as the head of one of the greatest religious houses in the land with gusto, managing the accounts, solving disputes between the nuns and making sure that all was in order and all was Christ-focussed.

But despite the fact that her illness had abated, Werburgh's strength did not return to what it had previously been and when the harsh winter began to set in she fell ill again, this time more serious than the last, taking to her bed and on the verge of death for weeks.

But again prayers and inner strength shone through and whilst the days were at their shortest Werburgh again improved and when the Twelve Days of Christmas finished and the Feast of Epiphany was upon them she was again walking about and almost back to full strength.

But as she prayed during those long dark winter hours Werburgh knew that her days on this earth were numbered and that, like Christ Himself in the Garden of Gethsemane, she was being asked to prepare for the end. "But how and where?" she asked the Lord, but before she'd even finished asking the question she knew; a vision of the fast-flowing waters of the Dove downstream from her blessed brother's hermitage filled her head and there and then she fixed her mind on Heánbyrig, her favourite of all the priories that she'd established.

After Epiphany Werburgh set out, saying nothing to the sisters of the true purpose behind her trip, instead making out that the journey was a purely pastoral one. And in some ways it was, for she visited Weedon and Stone where she knelt by the graves of her martyred brothers on the way. But travelling through the driving rain from Rufin's tomb to the priory at Trenthamm she fell ill again, the fever covering her brow and causing her to faint as she rode, the servants carrying her to her bed in the priory.

The good sisters, Wulfryn, Æmma and Cwenburgh amongst them, nursed their Holy Mother, but Werburgh knew that this was it; she could hear the Lord calling her from this earthly existence and feel His presence in the room. "I so wanted to die by the Dove," she murmured to Him, trying to solicit one last favour. "Werburgh, by Dove, Trent or Jordan, what does it matter?" He replied, His brilliance and beauty filling the room. "In Heaven all the rivers are far more beautiful than these and because of your faith in Me, you have a place prepared there for all eternity. On earth you shall always be in a foreign land, now my dear daughter, it is time for you to return home."

And in that dark room, the pious sisters knelt by her bedside, candles flickering in the night, Werburgh got up, took the hand of that King of Kings and the mother of Mercia left this life and a sweet smell filled the air, the smell of purity, of piety, of a saint who had returned home.

But even though she had left, Werburgh also remained, for within days of her death miracles began to be performed in her name and so it has continued until this day where she is still remembered in the great cathedral built around her shrine at Chester and whenever a good Christian Mercian sees a flock of wild geese fly overhead.

*11th September, 2012*
*Written at the Shrine of St. Bertram, Ilam; the Shrine of St. Werburgh, Chester; the Shrine of St. Chad, Lichfield; St. Rufin's Chapel, Burston, St. Werburgh's Church, Hanbury, HMP Dovegate and Smallthorne*

# Appendix I: Writing a Life: Reconciling myth, history, geography and faith

St. Werburgh was the second Saxon saint that I have attempted to write a Life of after her (possible) brother St. Bertram, and the task was infinitely harder than the first. Bertram, you see, is a colourful character: he journeys to Ireland, elopes with a beautiful princess, slays wolves, battles with the Devil and wins a battle with the help of an angel whilst also healing people from magical wells and founding the town of Stafford. Compared to that, the life of a nun who founded monasteries and brought a goose back to life can seem rather dull and it is this dullness that made writing this Life both difficult and necessary.

One thing that was easier though, was the history. More is recorded about Werburgh than Bertram, (for whom there is virtually nothing), although that in itself makes the task rather hard in a certain fashion for one needs to try and fit her into all the places she is meant to have been in within the timescale allowed, whilst also bringing to life a life of bureaucratic excellence.

We know that Werburgh was the daughter of King Wulfhere of Mercia and Queen – later St. – Ermenilda, herself of royal blood, coming from the Kingdom of Kent. King Wulfhere presents us with a number of problems for, like with so many Saxons, different and often conflicting stories are told about him. What we know is that he was King of Mercia from 658 until his death in 675. We know that he was one of the first Christian kings of Mercia but the details of his conversion from Paganism are disputed. We know that he was baptised and that his wife was a Christian but that is all. One version states that he was baptised before ascending to the throne, (under Christian Northumbrian influence), and continued as a good and Christian king throughout, whilst another agrees that he was baptised early on solely for political reasons, but then reverted to Paganism to garner support for throwing out Mercia's Northumbrian overlords and then ruled as a fierce and staunch Pagan until his conversion under St. Chad following the deaths of his sons Rufin and Wulfad. It is this second version that I have followed.

Sts. Wulfad and Rufin are little known even in Staffordshire, both only remembered in one church each, Wulfad sharing the dedication with St. Michael of Stone's parish church,[5] (where he was slain – the name of the town comes from the stone laid to mark the spot), whilst Rufin is remembered in the tiny Victorian chapel near his former shrine, a minor place of pilgrimage up until the Reformation. Some historians doubt the two ever actually existed; most consider them to have been unconnected with the historical King Wulfhere. The legends state however, that they became Christians after chancing upon St. Chad in his hermitage near to Salt and were betrayed by Wulfhere's general Werbode who was angry because their sister, Werburgh, refused his advances, wishing to wed only Christ. The legend also states that after their martyrdoms and Wulfhere's subsequent return to the faith, Werbode was seized with madness and died a terrible and paintful death. True or not, I found the figure of an angry and stubborn man who killed his own sons because he was too proud to accept they had minds of their own, too powerful and relevant to modern Britain with its 'honour killings' and other such tragedies, to remain hidden. Wulfhere resounds across the ages because he has flaws which we all show from time to time and I found it thought-provoking to consider how those rash actions of a stubborn man might affect, not him or the martyred sons, but instead the innocent sister of the fallen. Writing about Werburgh mourning over her brother's corpse just metres away from where it happened in the simple yet moving Chapel of St. Rufin at Burston was a powerful experience.

Unlike with Wulfad and Rufin, we know for sure that Werburgh was Wulfhere's daughter for it is recorded in the chronicles. They tell us about two children of Wulfhere: Werburgh and Conrad (Cœnrad), the boy who later succeeded Æthelred as King of Mercia, although there was possibly another, Berhtwald who I have identified as being one and the same as Bertram, the saint who is recorded as being a 'Prince of Stafford'. We know that she left Wulfherecester to take the veil at Ely Abbey under her grandmother, St. Æthelthryth – also know as St. Audrey, another popular Saxon saint and it is from her that the term 'tawdry' is derived for goods sold at the market on her feast day were said to be of a poor quality – and the after she died, Werburgh's grandmother St. Seaxburgh took over the position, then her mother St. Ermenilda and then finally Werburgh herself.

---

[5] Even this is only a recent development as the church was previously dedicated solely to St. Michael and it was only in the 21st century that St. Wulfad was included because of his connections with the site.

However, Werburgh is far more famous for her work in Mercia. As in my Life, she is recalled to the kingdom by King Æthelred – who succeeded her father Wulfhere after his death – in order to establish priories and other religious institutions. It is not known however, whether this was after she was made Abbess of Ely or before and in my Life I made it before as I found the most challenging and relevant part of writing Werburgh's story was in how she adapted from being a secluded nun into a worldly and capable administrator.

In our post-modern times, young virgins who give up the world to become nuns may seem a bit irrelevant, certainly out-of-synch with how the majority of our women today live. But whilst that may hold true, when writing about Werburgh in her role as the spreader of the Gospel in these parts, then to me it was a lesson straight out of our times and as relevant today as it was five hundred years ago if not more, for these days many young women do find themselves in positions of power and Werburgh can be a good guide to them – and some of us men – in how to fulfil those roles.

Of all the things on earth, none corrupt men and women so much as power. Good and holy people can become tempted by worldly wealth and influence, by the prospect of fulfilling an overall good by causing wrong to others, and so lose their very souls. I see it when I carry out my job everyday in both others and myself. Have we not all been tempted to bend a rule here and there, do a 'favour' for a 'mate' in order to get something in return? But is this the Way of Christ or is it the way of the Devil? Werburgh however, shines as an example to us all even from those far off times. Because she actively sought to humble herself, divest herself of power and status, she was the ideal person to wield both in a Christian manner. She took on the duty assigned to her by God even though she didn't really want it, but she gave it her all and her legacy is still with us today.

We do not know exactly which institutions were founded by Werburgh and which not although Trentham, Hanbury and Weedon are all cited as being definitely the fruit of her labours. There is however, an issue with the latter, for I have read different sources stating different things about Weedon. Most state that it was near to Chester but some that it was in Northamptonshire. Since both were in Mercia, then both are possible, but wherever the true place was, to my knowledge, nothing remains today. Similarly, there is nothing at either Hanbury or Trentham, although both parish churches are located on the site of the priory churches and the one at Hanbury is dedicated to Werburgh.

As for the other institutions, we are in the land of conjecture. Strangely, the priory at Stone founded on the place of St. Wulfad's martyrdom, is never attributed to Werburgh, but interestingly, the abbey at Repton is said by some to have been hers with her being recorded as the first abbess. If this is the case then she has surely left an enduring legacy in that place, for it produced two more saints, St. Guthlac and St. Wystan and remains of the institution are still with us today in the form of the fantastic Saxon crypt of the parish church of St. Wystan, whilst the famous Repton School occupies many of the former monastic buildings and is entered through the mediæval abbey gateway.

Where artistic license and pure fiction have entered this Life though, is regards to Ilam. There is no record of Werburgh ever going there and sitting with her brother Bertram, nor that a priory was ever considered in that place, but the temptation of linking these two fascinating saints was too great for me to ignore. Imagining them, brother and sister, sat side by side outside Bertram's humble hermitage, the bubbling waters of the Manifold flowing by the door, both servants of Christ yet in two very different ways, was to me a beautiful vision and writing part of this book at the Shrine of St. Bertram helped bring it to life.

What is recorded however, is that Werburgh wished to die at Hanbury but instead she passed away at Trentham. That is where this Life ends, but in fact, with Werburgh in many ways it is where the story begins, for after her death the sisters of Hanbury came to claim her body but the sisters at Trentham refused to give it up and set up extensive security arrangements to prevent its theft. However, Werburgh must have evidently been watching down with distaste from on high, for it is written that all the bolts sprang open and the guards fell into a deep sleep so the body was spirited away to her beloved Hanbury where it stayed for almost two hundred years until 860 when it was relocated to Chester due to the fear of Danish raids, Chester's Church of St. Peter and St. Paul being within the safety of the Roman city walls.

Soon afterwards that church became Chester Cathedral and was rededicated to St. Werburgh and St. Oswald – the Northumbrian king who first Christianised Mercia – and over the years the popularity of St. Werburgh's Shrine grew so that thousands of pilgrims sought her prayers annually and her cult spread across England with churches being dedicated to her all over the land and settlements being named in her honour in such far off places as Kent and Bristol. Nowadays, her fame is even international, with churches dedicated to her in Ireland, Australia and even Zimbabwe!

St. Werburgh's cult and shrine however, were destroyed during Henry VIII's Dissolution of the Monasteries and the elaborate shrine constructed in the 14th century was destroyed by the reformers. However, in 1876 the various pieces were collected together by one A. W. Blomfield and the shrine reconstructed. To this day it still stands, in the heart of Chester's glorious cathedral, as a reminder to all of the simple Christian lady who became the spiritual mother of Mercia.

*St. Werburgh's Shrine, Chester Cathedral*

# Appendix II: St. Werburgh Pilgrimage

Christians wishing to honour and get to know St. Werburgh better by undertaking a pilgrimage will be pleased to know that there are several sites connected with her that are well worth visiting and that her shrine is now part of a recognised and signposted pilgrimage route, the Two Saints Way which runs between her shrine at Chester to St. Chad's Shrine at Lichfield. This route, which visits several holy sites connected with not only Werburgh and Chad but also several others saints, (including Wulfad, Rufin and Bertram), is almost ninety miles long and is backed up with some excellent resources. Visit the website here: www.twosaintsway.org.uk

For those without the time, energy or ability to walk almost ninety miles, then St. Werburgh's Shrine at Chester Cathedral is the obvious place to start. Located behind the main altar, the 14th century shrine which was destroyed during the Reformation was pieced together in the 19th century and reinstated. Recently a small statue of St. Werburgh was added to the shrine. Visitors may also be interested to learnt that the adjacent side chapel is also dedicated to her. Whilst visiting, stop and meditate awhile and the legacy of St. Werburgh after her death, on the thousands who have come to pray at that place and who have been blessed by miracles in her name. Meditate too, since legend states that it happened near to Chester, on the Legend of the Geese and what God was trying to teach us through that miracle. Pray for all of God's creatures no matter how simple or humble and pray that we may treat them all with the respect and love that they deserve as creations of the Almighty.

Chester Cathedral has a website which contains details of service times and admission fees as well as the other delights of this ancient building: http://www.chestercathedral.com/

Whilst visiting cathedrals, one should also try to take a trip down to Ely Cathedral. This is a marvellous building in its own right and in the heart of a wonderful old city, but it is important to us because it stands on the site of the abbey where Werburgh spent so many years as a nun and then later, as the fourth abbess. She is, of course, far from being the only saint associated with the site and whilst here prayers should also be offered to her mother, St.

Ermenilda, the third abbess, her grandmother, St. Seaxburgh, the second abbess and the first abbess and founder of the abbey, St. Æthelthryth, (also referred to as Ethelreda, Editrudis and Audrey), St. Werburgh's great aunt. Indeed, it is this last saint who deserves the most attention at Ely for she was the first in a great family of saints and her shrine stood in the cathedral up until the Reformation. Although that was sadly destroyed, a statue of her erected later serves as her shrine and a focus for our prayers whilst her hand is preserved at the nearby Roman Catholic church. Whilst at Ely meditate on the influence that the females of her family had on St. Werburgh, how they nurtured her and loved her. Meditate too on how Our Lady did the same for Christ up to and including standing at the foot of the cross as He suffered and visiting His tomb. Pray for all mothers, aunts and grandmothers, particularly your own who have made you the person that you are today.

The website is: http://www.elycathedral.org/

Returning to Staffordshire, other sites worthy of visiting have to be Trentham Parish Church and St. Werburgh's at Hanbury since both these churches occupy the sites of the former priory churches in the institutions that she founded and both, like Chester Cathedral, are places where her remains reposed for some time, with Hanbury being a noted place of pilgrimage prior to her body being transferred to Chester in 875. Sadly, neither church is remotely original. Trentham's dates only from the 19th century as part of the rebuilding of Trentham Hall, (which once stood connected to it at the back), but there is still a tangible link with Werburgh in the form of a Saxon preaching cross in the churchyard. Trentham church itself is renowned locally for its charismatic style and evangelical flavour which may seem a bit at odds with the veneration of saints – certainly asking St. Werburgh to pray for you is not a common activity there these days – but conversely, one might sit by the cross that could have been planted in her lifetime and wonder if she was not the charismatic evangelist of her day with the same core message as the modern-day church at Trentham, that of bringing the message of Christ to a largely non-Christian world.

Trentham's website is http://www.trenthamchurch.org.uk/ and the church can be reached by turning off the A34 at the first set of traffic lights north of the Trentham Gardens roundabout, (left if coming from the south, right if from the north), and then turn left and the church is ahead of you at the end of the road. N.B. Although adjacent to the famous Trentham Gardens, there is no access to the church from them and vice versa.

*Trentham Parish Church with its Saxon Preaching Cross*

Visiting St. Werburgh's at Hanbury is a very different experience. Unlike Trentham which is hidden until you are right next to it, St. Werburgh's occupies a headland overlooking the broad plain of the Dove and can be seen for miles around. The Saxon church was probably wooden and was destroyed in a Danish raid around 875 and the building that we see today dates largely from the 14th century with some Victorian additions, (including the delightful statue of St. Werburgh in a niche on the tower). Inside the church is spectacular, the murals on the walls of the chancel and sanctuary depicting the life of Christ being really worth seeing, but our interests lie to the right where there is a fine stained-glass window depicting the patron saint of the church and a banner of her as well. This serves best as a focus for our prayers and so kneel awhile here and meditate on her work at Hanbury, her wish to die there and the many years when her remains reposed in this place.

St. Werburgh's does not have a website but this site provides some excellent information and photos: http://www.themcs.org/churches/Hanbury%20-%20St%20Werburgh.html St. Werburgh's can be reached by turning off the A50 at the Sudbury roundabout and taking the A515 over the Dove, then turning left at the roundabout and then the first right.

*Stained glass window of St. Werburgh, Hanbury*

Another site in the vicinity of Hanbury well worth visiting is St. Wystan's Church in Repton. Dedicated to another Saxon saint and with connections to a third, St. Guthlac, St. Wystan's is a gem both in its pedigree and present-day remains. Repton was, for a time, the capital of Mercia and the site of an important abbey which, it is said, St. Werburgh founded. The site of the abbey – later destroyed by Danes, then rebuilt in the 12th century and destroyed for a second time during the Reformation – is now the famous public school. There is little connected to St. Werburgh in the church itself, but a trip down into the miraculously preserved Saxon crypt is a must, for nowhere else evokes the feeling of Werburgh's Mercia more than here. The crypt was also the site of the Shrine of St. Wystan so pray awhile here and meditate on the life of that saint, a martyr for the faith who died in 849.

St. Wystan's website is to be found here http://www.reptonchurch.org.uk/ and the church can be reached by turning off the A50 at the A38 junction and taking the turn signposted 'Repton'. The church is by the road on your left as you enter Repton village.

The last site of interest connected with St. Werburgh is that of Burybank, once the royal citadel of Wulfherecester where she was born and raised. Burybank is just off the A34 north of Stone. To get there from Stafford, simple take the A34 north (signposted Stoke-on-Trent), taking a left at the roundabout with the Darlaston Arms pub in its centre. The hillfort is just on the right and although there are no public footpaths running over it, locals do walk their dogs there. Near to Burybank are two Saxon burial lowes, perhaps belonging to Wulfhere and another relative of Werburgh. Here's the link:   http://www.megalithic.co.uk/article.php?sid=4981

Finally, since this book also deals in detail with the martyrdoms of Sts. Rufin and Wulfad, why not take a trip to the Church of St. Michael and St. Wulfad in Stone and the Chapel of St. Rufin in Burston, both of which are built on the sites of their martyrdoms. Whilst both are post-Reformation, Stone church has the remains of a Saxon preaching cross in its churchyard which may serve as a focus for your devotions whilst near to St. Rufin's is a holy well dedicated to that saint.

St. Michael and St. Wulfad's: http://www.stmichaelschurchstone.co.uk/category/places/st-michael-st-wulfads

St. Rufin's Well: http://www.megalithic.co.uk/article.php?sid=17154.

*The Church of St. Michael and St. Wulfad, Stone, with the remains of the Saxon preaching cross in the foreground*